English for Tourism

Tourist Information & Creative Thinking for Language Learners

Myeong-Hee Seong

지식인공동체 지식인

Profile

Myeong-Hee Seong
Ph.D. in English Education, Korea University
Professor, Eulji University

English for Tourism

Tourist Information & Creative Thinking for Language Learners

2015년 3월 10일 초판 1쇄 인쇄
2015년 3월 13일 초판 1쇄 발행

지은이 | Myeong-Hee Seong
펴낸이 | 김종욱
펴낸곳 | 지식인공동체 지식인
등 록 | 제301-2013-134호
주 소 | 서울시 도봉구 도봉로 476, 415호(삼성쉐르빌퍼스티)
전 화 | 02)2266-8606
팩 스 | 02)2266-8607
E-mail | jisikin2013@naver.com

ISBN 978-89-98591-41-0 (93740)

값 13,000원

English for Tourism

Tourist Information & Creative Thinking for Language Learners

CONTENTS

CHAPTER 1

China

China, Cultural Treasure-house of East Asia

Unit 1

Vocabulary & Grammar Practice

[1] Which of the following best completes the sentences?

The weather in China is extremely various. Great differences in climate are found from region to region owing to China's (   ) territory and complex topography.

a) intensive
b) extensive
c) high
d) narrow

[2] Unscramble the words to find the correct definitions for the words below.

a) southernmost: south, farthest

➜

b) ethnic: of, race

➜

c) diverse: kind, a, of, different

➜

d) population: number, area, people, a particular, living, of, in

➜

e) census: population, process, official, country's, of, an, counting, a

➜

f) aesthetic: beauty, connected, with

➜

g) substantial: amount or number, enough, large, noticeable, in, to, be

➜

h) territory: land, district, or

➜

i) topography: the river, road, building, position, etc., of

➜

j) temperate: extremes, free, from

➜

[3] Match each word in the first column with its meaning in the second column.

a) southernmost •	• a) an official process of counting a country's population
b) ethnic •	• b) large enough in amount or number to be noticeable
c) diverse •	• c) connected with beauty and the study of beauty
d) population •	• d) moderate
e) census •	• e) land or district
f) aesthetic •	• f) position of the rivers, roads, buildings, etc
g) substantial •	• g) (number of) people living in a particular area, country, etc,
h) territory •	• h) farthest south
i) topography •	• i) of race, of a particular cultural group
j) temperate •	• j) various

Reading or Listening Practice

[1] Think about the following questions.

1. Name the countries around China.

____

2. Name the different peoples that make up China's population.

____

3. What is the major religion in china?

____

4. What is the major language in China?

____

5. Name the tourist attractions in China.

____

[2] Read or listen to the following passages and answer the above questions.

China, Cultural Treasure-house of East Asia

China is located in Eastern Asia, bordering the East China Sea, Korea Bay, Yellow Sea, and South China Sea, between North Korea and Vietnam. With the total land area of about 9,326,410 square kilometers, China is slightly smaller than the United States and is the world's fourth-largest country (after Russia, Canada, and US). In China, there are 6,536 islands larger than 500 square meters, the largest being Taiwan, with a total area of about 36,000 square kilometers, and the second largest is Hainan. The South China Sea Islands are the southernmost island group of China. The majority of China's people live in the eastern segment of the country.

China is a country with 56 nationalities, including the Han, the Manchu, the Mongol, the Uygur, the Zhuang, the Tibetan and so on. China's ethnically diverse population is the largest in the world. When China conducted its first population census in 1982, China was a nation of more than 1 billion people, or about one-fifth of the world's populations. These nationalities are distributed all over China and form diversified folk cultures due to the varying natural and social environment they live in. The Han people make up over 90 percent of the total population. Members of non-Han groups, referred to as the "minority nationalities," constitute about 10 percent of the total population but number more than 70 million people. The different customs are of great aesthetic value.

Different ethnic groups usually follow different religions, so China is a multi-religious country. Buddhism, Taoism and Islam are the three major religions. Catholicism and Protestantism have smaller but substantial followers, too. On the whole, however, religion has not been a major issue in China.

In languages, both Putonghua (the dialect of Mandarin as spoken in Beijing) and English are the languages of business. So, if the foreigners travel to China for business purposes, they can usually communicate with the Chinese merchants in simple English. However, Putonghua is an official language of China. Most of the Chinese merely speak Putonghua with the outsiders. So, if the foreign tourists want to visit China but cannot speak Putonghua, they will find traveling in China inconvenient. Therefore, it is highly recommended for the foreign tourists to learn some simple Putonghua when they decide to visit China.

The weather in China is extremely diverse. Great differences in climate are found from region to region owing to China's extensive territory and complex topography. Although most of the country lies in the temperate zone, southern areas are in the tropical or subtropical zone while northern areas are in the frigid zone. For instance, Northern Heilongjiang Province, China's northernmost point, has a winter climate year round without summer, while Hainan Island, its southernmost point, has a summer climate the year round without winter. In general, the temperature in China in the winter is 5 to 18 degrees centigrade lower than that in other countries on the same latitude in winter.

There are many tourist attractions in China. With a 3,000-year history, Beijing has been the capital city of China since the Ming dynasty (1368-1644). After more than 700 years, the historical sites – the Forbidden City, the Temple of Heaven, the Summer Palace and the Great Wall are still maintained in good shape. Every year visitors from around the world come to visit Beijing to experience ancient China's art and culture and today's modern urban life. Shanghai, the largest city of China, is located on the east coast of China and is the gateway of the Yangze River basin. For centuries Shanghai has been a comprehensive industrial base and an important port for China-international trade. Hong Kong became the Special Administrative Region (SAR) of China on 1 July 1997. Despite the change of leadership from British rule to Chinese, Hong Kong remains one of the world's most important economic centers and one of the most popular vacation destinations on the earth.

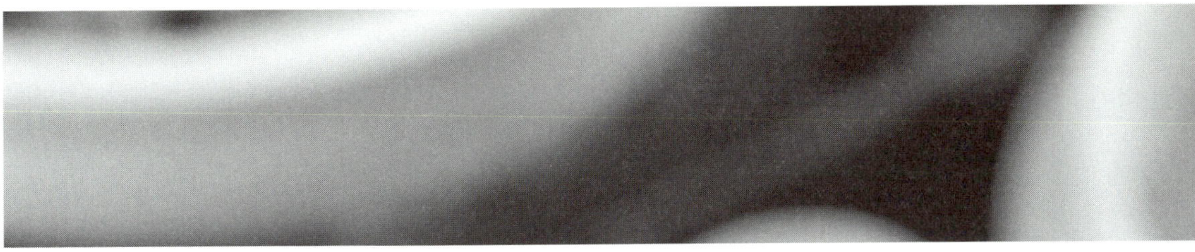

China CHAPTER 1

Shopping & Food in China

Unit 2

Vocabulary & Grammar Practice

[1] Which of the following is closest to the meaning of the underlined word?

Whereas foods from Canton are delicate, in Sichuan food the tastes are strong and dramatic

a) dishes
b) flavors
c) sauces
d) dressings

[2] Which of the following best completes the sentences?

Sichuan food is the (   ) food of China, where pepper and chili really get into the act

a) very sweet
b) very hot
c) very sour
d) very bitter

[3] Match each word in the first column with its meaning in the second column.

a) craft •	• a) a job needing skill, esp. with one's hands
b) inheritance •	• b) to make or become greater in number or quantity
c) embroidery •	• c) money, property that you receive from someone who has died
d) pottery •	• d) to give something a different color using a dye
e) dyeing •	• e) a very good copy especially of a painting or other work of art
f) replica •	• f) a decoration or pattern made by sewing onto cloth
g) exquisitely •	• g) extremely beautifully, excellently
h) relic •	• h) object made out of baked clay
i) accumulate •	• i) something old that reminds us of the past
j) liquor •	• j) an alcoholic drink

Reading or Listening Practice

[1] Think about the following questions.

1. *List products that can be purchased in China.*

2. *Name foods you can enjoy in China.*

3. *Write the key points, based on what you heard (read) from the below passages.*

[2] Read or listen to the following passages and answer the above questions.

China Shopping & Dining

China is a treasure house of arts and crafts which are an important part of the Nation's cultural inheritance. Products such as carving, embroidery, pottery, dyeing, and replicas of ancient cultural relics are all exquisitely crafted. Other famous Chinese products include silk, tea, liquors and traditional Chinese medicine.

China is also the home of tea. Tea is divided into green, black, perfumed, white and Wulong tea. Longjing (green tea) and Biluochun (green tea) are famous throughout the world. And China's liquors have developed in their own unique way and have won many international awards. There are many famous liquors such as Maotai. Traditional Chinese medicine is famous throughout the world as well. The body of knowledge that makes up traditional Chinese medicine has been accumulated over thousands of years. Numerous herbal and other drugs are being used for their high curative efficacy, and those with a high tonic value are favorites with the Chinese.

Chinese food enjoys a high reputation in the world not only for its delicious taste and charming appearance but also for its abundance. It is due to the diversity of the climate, products and customs that there are widely different food styles and tastes in local regions.

Beijing food is the most famous food of China, particularly known for Beijing (Peking) Duck. Thin slices of the skin are cut off and put onto a plate where it is wrapped with a fresh flour tortilla with plum sauce, cucumber, and green onion. Some find it a bit too greasy, but others get hooked after one taste. In any case, a Beijing Duck dinner is usually a fixed item on any Beijing tour itinerary.

Cantonese food or Guangdong food, another famous food of China, typically is steamed, boiled or stir-fried. It is a very healthy food since it uses a minimum amount of oil. The main ingredients of this type of Chinese food are seafood, pork, chicken and vegetables, but could include almost anything. You need white rice to accompany the meal to make it complete unless it is a special banquet. It is said, "the Cantonese eat every thing that flies except planes, every thing on the ground except cars, and every thing that is in water except boats."

Sichuan food is the fiery food of China, where pepper and chili really get into the act. Whereas foods from Canton are delicate, in Sichuan food the flavors are strong and dramatic. The most famous Sichuan dish is the Gongbao (Kung Pao) chicken, fried with peanuts and chili pepper. Many Sichuan dishes are prepared using chili pepper oil, which gives a special taste to the food.

English for Tourism

Tourist Information & Creative Thinking for Language Learners

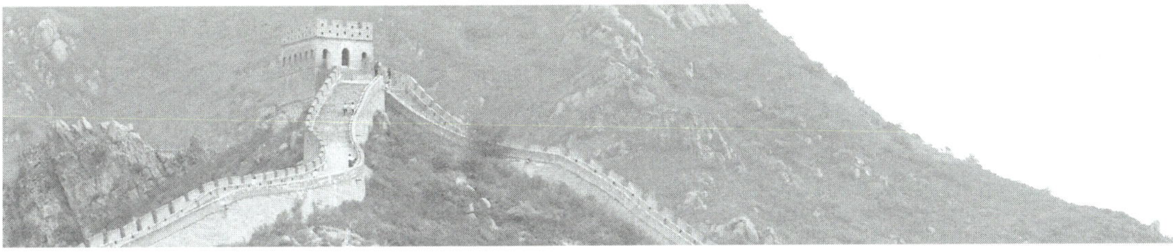

China

CHAPTER 1

Tourist Attractions | Unit 3

Vocabulary Practice

Which word does the following definition refer to?

1. *to give up the position of being king or queen*

a) abdicate
b) throne
c) abode
d) successive

2. *a political system in which one country rules a lot of other countries*

a) feudalism
b) imperialism
c) democracy
d) communism

3. *to keep someone or something safe from harm or damage*

a) repair
b) protect
c) provid
d) prevent

4. *lodgings, accommodations*

a) quarters
b) beam
c) enclave
d) garment

5. *moderate*

a) hazy
b) temperate
c) numerous
d) rare

Speaking Practice

How do you say the following in English?

1. 상하이는 중국의 동해안에 위치해 있다.

2. 중국의 동해안에 위치해 있는 상하이는 중국에서 가장 인구가 많은 도시이다.

3. 자금성은 명(Ming)과 청(Qing) 왕조 동안 황제의 궁전이었다.

4. 명, 청 왕조 동안 황제의 궁전이었던 자금성은 세계에서 가장 큰 궁전이다.

5. 만리장성은 세계에서 가장 경이스러운 것 중에 하나로 여겨지고 있다.

6. 세계에서 가장 경이스러운 것 중에 하나로 여겨지는 만리장성은 유네스코에 의해 1987년에 세계문화유산에 등재되었다.

7. 이하원은 중국에서 가장 잘 보존되어있는 왕실의 정원이다.

8. 중국에서 가장 잘 보존되어 있는 왕실 정원인 이하원은 예전에 청왕조 황제의 여름 거주지였다.

9–10. 중국인들은 비행기를 빼고 나는 모든 것을, 차를 제외하고 땅에 있는 모든 것을, 배를 빼고 물에 있는 모든 것을 먹는다고들 한다.

Reading or Listening Practice

Beijing

Beijing, situated in the northeastern part of China, is the capital of the People's Republic of China and has been the heart and soul of politics and society throughout its long history. It was known as Peking by the cradle of China's new democratic revolution. The May Fourth Movement against imperialism and feudalism began here in 1919.

The climate in Beijing is of the continental type, with cold and dry winters and hot summers. The best time to visit Beijing is May, September and October, when people enjoy bright sunny sky.

Famous Beijing attractions include the Forbidden City, the Great Wall, and Tian'anmen Square. Seated at the very heart of Beijing, Tian'anmen Square was originally designed in 1651 and it was quadrupled in size in 1958. Now it covers an area of 40.5 hectares and can hold up to one million people; thus, it is one of the largest public squares in the world. It is surrounded by several impressive structures. The oldest of these is the Tian'anmen Gate to the north. To the east are the Museums of Chinese History and Revolution, to the west the Great Hall of the People and to the south the Chairman Mao Memorial Hall. In the middle of the square is the monument of the People's Heroes. Tian'anmen Square has often been the scene of big demonstrations, mass meetings, parades and celebrations since it was built.

Now known as the Palace Museum, the Forbidden City is to the north of Tian'anmen Square. It is the world's largest palace complex and covers 74 hectares. Surrounded by a six meter deep moat and a ten meter high wall are 9,999 buildings. It is divided into two parts. The southern section, or the Outer Court was where the emperor exercised his supreme power over the nation.

The northen section, or the Inner Court was where he lived with his royal family.

The Forbidden City was the imperial palace during the Ming and Qing Dynasties. It is the largest and most well preserved imperial residence in China today. Under Ming Emperor Yongle, construction began in 1406. It took 14 years to build the Forbidden City. The first ruler who actually lived here was Ming Emperor Zhudi. For five centuries thereafter, it continued to be the residence of 23 successive emperors until 1911 when Qing Emperor Puyi was forced to abdicate the throne.

In Chinese, the Forbidden City is called Purple Forbidden City. "Purple" does not refer to the color of the buildings or walls, but has a mythological origin. It is said that the Emperor of Heaven has his palaces in the region of the North Star, of which purple is the symbolic color. The abode of the temporal emperor, therefore, is supposed to have the same color. Having been the imperial palace for some five centuries, it houses numerous rare treasures and curiosities. Listed by UNESCO as a World Cultural Heritage Site in 1987, the Palace Museum is now one of the most popular tourist attractions worldwide.

The Great Wall

The Great Wall, the world's largest military structure, is considered one of the greatest wonders in the world and it was enlisted in the World Heritage by UNESCO in 1987. Construction of the Wall first began during the period of the Warring States (476-221 BC). Formerly, walls were built at strategic points by different kingdoms to protect their northern territories. In 211 BC after the first emperor of the Qin Dynasty unified China, he decided to have the walls linked up and extended them to more than 10,000 li or 5,000 kilometers. This is the origin of the name of the 10,000-li Great Wall.

After that, the Great Wall went through constant extensions and repairs in later dynasties. The Wall we see today is almost exactly the result of this effort. With a total length of over 6,000 kilometers, it extends to the Jiayu Pass in Gansu Province in the west and to the mouth of the Yalu River in Liaoning Province in the east. The Great Wall is a series of walls built and rebuilt by different dynasties over 1,000 years.

The Summer Palace

Located 15 km from Beijing, the Summer Palace is the best preserved and the second largest royal garden in China. It used to be a summer residence of Qing Dynasty emperors and is now a public park. All the man-made hills, pavilions and temples, including Kunming Lake and Longevity Hall, blend together harmoniously in spite of their individual styles.

The Summer Palace was first named the Garden of Clear Ripples, which was burnt down by the allied forces of Great Britain and France in 1860. Reconstruction started 25 years later and was completed in 1895, and the name was changed to Yiheyuan (Garden of Good Health and Harmony).

The main features of the Summer Palace are Kunming Lake and Longevity Hill. Like most imperial palaces in China, the Summer Palace is divided into three parts: halls for political affairs, living quarters and religious buildings. The most important structures of the Summer Palace are Painting Walkway, the longest walkway in the Chinese gardens with altogether over 14,000 traditional Chinese paintings on the beams and crossbeams, and Marble Boat, which was built for the 50th birthday celebration of Dowager Empress Ci'x, and where one can enjoy the hazy scene over the lake in rainy days.

Shanghai

Situated in the middle of east China's coast, Shanghai, literally "the City on the Sea," is the largest and most populous city in the country. Shanghai is China's main center for industry, commerce, foreign trade, science and technology, ranking no. 1 in population density and as a seaport.

Shanghai is well known both at home and abroad not only for its prosperous metropolitan feature and rich humanistic resources but also for a number of tourist attractions with modern flavor that have been developed in recent years. Varied and colorful tourist festivities like the Shanghai Tourism Festival, the New Year Eve Longhua Temple Bell Striking, the Longhua Temple Fair, the Nanhui County Peach Blossom Festival, the International Tea Culture Festival, the Sweet Osmanthus Festival and the Orange Festival are attracting an even increasing number of domestic and foreign tourists.

Shanghai enjoys a delightful climate with four distinct seasons. Annual temperatures average 16℃ and annual rainfall averages 1,200 millimeters. However, spring and autumn, with their moderate temperature, are the best times to visit Shanghai.

English for Tourism
Tourist Information & Creative Thinking for Language Learners

Thailand

CHAPTER 2

Thailand, the 'Land of Smiles'

Unit 1

Vocabulary & Grammar Practice

[1] Which of the following is closest to the meaning of the underlined word?

> There are three seasons: the cool season from November to February, the hot season from April to May, and the rainy season from June to October, though downpours rarely <u>continue</u> more than a couple of hours.

a) stop　　b) happen

c) last　　d) comprise

[2] Unscramble the words to find the correct definitions for the words below.

a) infertile: of, incapable, producing

→

b) rural: a countryside, of

→

c) urban: a town or city, of

→

d) fertile: to produce, able, crops, good

→

e) counterfeit: that, to look like, is made, the original one, something

→

f) celadon: a pale green glaze, pottery, a type, having, of

→

g) cuisine: cooking, of, a style

→

h) vendor: things, sells, who, someone

→

i) gem: a special shape, into, cut, has been, that, a beautiful stone

→

j) arid: dry, extremely

→

[3] Match each word in the first column with its meaning in the second column.

a) diversity •	• a) of a racial group
b) ethnic •	• b) variety
c) homogeneous •	• c) a variety of a language spoken only in one area
d) dialect •	• d) of or like the countryside
e) rural •	• e) of or in a town or city
f) urban •	• f) a member of an all-male religious group that lives apart from other people
g) tone •	• g) the best or most suitably
h) monk •	• h) the way your voice sounds
i) optimally •	• i) cooking, style of cooking
j) cuisine •	• j) of the same kind, uniform

Reading or Listening Practice

[1] Think about the following questions.

1. Name the countries around Thailand.

   ____

2. Which months are best for sightseeing in Thailand?

   ____

3. Name the different peoples that make up Thailand's population.

   ____

4. What is the major language in Thailand?

   ____

5. What is the major religion in Thailand?

   ____

[2] Read or listen to the following passages and answer the above questions.

Thailand, the 'Land of Smiles'

A unified Thai kingdom was established in the mid-14th century. It was known as Siam until 1939 and it boasts the distinction of being the only country in Southeast Asia never to have been colonized by a European power. The word "Thai" means "free," and therefore "Thailand" means "Land of the Free."

Geographically, the Kingdom of Thailand is located in the heart of Southeast Asia and shares boundaries with Myanmar (Burma) on the west and northwest, Laos on the east and northeast, Cambodia on the southeast, and Malaysia on the south. It comprises the flat, damp plains of the Chao Phraya river estuary, ideal for growing rice. It is divided into four distinct areas: the mountainous North, the fertile Central Plains, the semi-arid plateau of the Northeast, and the peninsula South, distinguished by its many beautiful tropical beaches and offshore islands.

Lying within the humid tropics, Thailand remains hot throughout the year. Average low temperature is about 20℃ and high temperature is 37℃. There are three seasons: the cool season from November to February, the hot season from April to May, and the rainy season from June to October, though downpours rarely last more than a couple of hours. The best time to go is from November through February, when the days are milder and the nights are cool. March through May is very hot, with temperatures reaching 38℃. Avoid mid-May through October, when it's humid and rainy.

The diversity of ethnic, linguistic, and religious groups is characteristic of most nations of Southeast Asia. However, Thailand's population is relatively homogeneous. More than 85% speak a dialect of Thai and share a common culture. Ethnic Thais form the majority. The largest minority is Chinese. Other minority groups include Malays, Cambodians, Indians, non-Thai hill tribes, and some Vietnamese. The population is mostly rural, concentrated in the rice-growing areas of the central, northeastern, and northern regions. However, as Thailand continues to industrialize, its urban population, principally in the Bangkok area, is growing.

The official national language of Thailand is Thai. Thai is a tone language. This means that different tones have different meanings. The Thai language has five tones, and if you mispronounce you do not simply say an incorrect word, you say another word entirely. Principal other languages are Chinese and Malay. English is a mandatory subject in public schools, and widely spoken and understood particularly in Bangkok and other major cities.

Thailand is one of the most strongly Buddhist countries in the world. Buddhism continues to cast strong influence on daily life. Every Thai male is expected to become a monk for a short period in his life, optimally between the time he finishes school and the time he starts a career or marries. The remainder of the population adheres to Islam, Christianity, Hinduism, and other faiths – all of which are allowed full freedom of expression.

Thailand is an easy country to travel in, with efficient transport, inexpensive accommodations and a delicious national cuisine. The Thais are renowned for their friendliness and hospitality to strangers. Thailand is equally well known for both its beach resorts and the shopping and night life of its busy cities. Popular destinations include the capital Bangkok, Chiangmai, and the resorts in Phuket, Koh Samui and Pattaya.

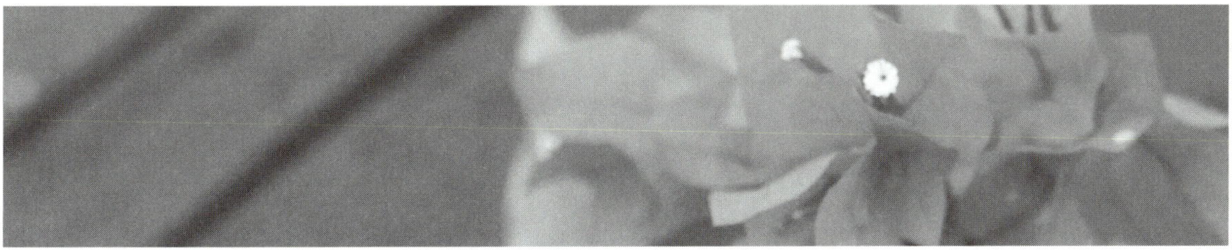

Thailand

CHAPTER 2

Shopping & Food in Thailand

Unit 2

Vocabulary & Grammar Practice

[1] Which of the following best completes the sentences?

Thailand owes its rich culinary arts to the (   ) of India, China, Malaysia and Indonesia.

a) cuisines
b) music
c) painting
d) religion

[2] Which of the following best completes the sentences?

The success of this country's cuisine lies in the (   ) of 4 basic tastes i.e. salty, sweet, sour and pungent.

a) mixture
b) pleasure
c) cuisine
d) cook

[3] Match each word in the first column with its meaning in the second column.

a) indigenous •	• a) native
b) virtually •	• b) almost, very nearly
c) gem •	• c) imitator
d) counterfeit •	• d) copy, imitation
e) copycat •	• e) a copy of a shape made by rubbing wax onto a piece of paper laid over
f) lacquer •	• f) vessels and other objects made of baked clay
g) celadon •	• g) a type of pottery having a pale green glaze
h) pottery •	• h) varnish used to give a hard, bright coating to metal
i) handicraft •	• i) work needing skill with the hands and artistic design
j) rubbing •	• j) jewel

Reading or Listening Practice

[1] **Think about the following questions.**

1. List products that can be purchased in Thailand.

2. Name foods you can enjoy in Thailand.

3. Write the key points, based on what you heard (read) from the below passages.

[2] Read or listen to the following passages and answer the above questions.

Thailand Shopping & Dining

Generally, shopping in Thailand is easy and fun. Bangkok is the colored gemstone capital of the world. Rubies and sapphires are indigenous stones, but virtually all colored gems, as well as diamonds, are available. Silk is a great buy in Bangkok, but there are a variety of qualities available. Other good shopping bargains are lacquer ware, celadon pottery, painted umbrellas, tribal weavings and handicrafts, temple rubbings, custom-made shoes and clothing, bronze, silver, gems, temple bells, and sand paintings. Bargaining is common in markets and with street vendors, but not in shops.

Thai food is internationally famous. Thailand owes its rich culinary arts to the cuisines of India, China, Malaysia and Indonesia. The success of this country's cuisine lies in the blend of 4 basic tastes i.e. salty, sweet, sour and pungent. Most dishes are masterfully balanced: They are hot, sweet, sour and spicy – all at the same time. The variety of vegetable and meat dishes is astonishing. Pork, poultry and some beef are used and seafood is outstanding.

Thailand is a paradise for tropical fruits. At any time during the year at least a dozen different kinds of fruits can be found in the market. These include the durians, rambutans, and mangosteens. Rambutans with soft spines on the outside taste like a sweet lemon. The mangoes are good in March through July. Mangosteens are another great-tasting tropical fruit. They are round with dark-brown skin, and are a little bigger than a golf ball. Inside is a sweet white fruit in segments, like an orange. Papayas and pomelos like a sweet grapefruit are also available. And if you can get past the smell, try the infamous durian fruit (It's so pungent that it's illegal to open one in your hotel room). There are more than 20 kinds of bananas. Thais eat them fresh, grilled and fried.

Thailand

CHAPTER 2

Tourist Attractions | Unit 3

Vocabulary Practice

Which word does the following definition refer to?

1. *very tall building*

   a) skyscraper   b) scale

   c) abode   d) attractions

2. *large cage or building for keeping birds*

   a) fence   b) cockpit

   c) abode   d) aviary

3. *provide a substitute for something*

   a) replace   b) inherit

   c) retain   d) give

4. *small-scale portrait, copy or model*

   a) landmark   b) miniature

   c) replications   d) plantation

5. *a large public garden where many different types of flowers and plants are grown*

   a) aquarium   b) aviary

   c) zoo   d) botanical garden

Speaking Practice

How do you say the following in English?

1. 태국은 시암(Siam)으로 알려졌었다.

2. 시암(Siam)으로 알려진 태국은 동남아시아의 중앙에 위치한다.

3. 방콕(Bangkok)은 태국의 수도로 설립되었다.

4. 태국의 수도로 설립된 방콕은 지리적으로 경제적으로 그 나라의 심장부이다.

5. 파타야(Pattaya)는 태국의 가장 큰 여행지 중 하나이다.

6. 태국에서 가장 큰 여행지 중의 하나인 Pattaya는 수상스포츠에 이상적인 곳이다.

7. 푸켓(Phuket)은 태국에서 가장 큰 섬이다.

8. 태국에서 가장 큰 섬인 Phuket은 관광하기에 아주 매력적이다.

9. 미니시암(Mini Siam)은 테마파크이다.

10. 테마파크인 Mini Siam에는 태국의 역사 유적과 사원의 축척 모형이 있다.

Reading or Listening Practice

Bangkok

Bangkok, Thailand's major gateway, is the Orient's most cosmopolitan city and has attractions to stimulate even the most jaded travellers. Created as the Thai capital in 1782 by the first monarch of the present Chakri dynasty, Bangkok holds the essence of the Thai spirit, and is very much the heart of the country, geographically, culturally and economically.

Bangkok is a modern capital, complete with gleaming skyscrapers. In the midst of dynamic modern growth, Bangkok embraces modern development and presents an initial picture of world-class hotels offering deluxe comforts such as glittering shopping plazas packed with treasures of the East such as silks and gemstones and restaurants serving Thailand's acclaimed spicy specialities and virtually every other national cuisine worthy of the name.

In the midst of dynamic modern growth, Bangkok miraculously manages to preserve its cultural heritage to a marked degree: the soaring roofs and gleaming spires of the Grand Palace and the city's many historic temples – the Temple of the Emerald Buddha, the Temple of Dawn and other evocative wonders.

Pattaya

Originally Pattaya was a small, unknown fishing village on the eastern side of Thailand facing the Gulf of Thailand. The tranquil fishermen's village disappeared and was replaced by shops, houses, mega-hotels, guest houses, department stores, and so on. It is only 147 kilometers away from Bangkok with a comfortable 3-hour drive. The transportation services to this resort are greatly convenient.

Pattaya, one of Thailand's biggest tourist destinations, attracts visitors from all over Thailand and overseas as well. For resort and leisure seekers, its sunny climate is an ideal place for swimming and sunbathing. The white sandy beaches are visited by sunbathers, not only from the local Thai but from foreign tourists around the world. There are three major beach areas, i.e. Pattaya Beach, Jomlien Beach and Coral Island. Numerous sporting activities can be found at this resort of Thailand. A full range of water sports are available including fishing, sailing, water skiing, windsurfing, scuba diving and parasailing.

Located only a 15 minute drive south of Pattaya, Nong Nooch Village is a must see for visitors to Pattaya. The village has beautiful tropical gardens and lakes. The cultural show is presented three times a day, with reproductions of traditional Thai ceremonies, dance, sword flighting and kick boxing. Within the mini zoo, there are aviaries for both birds and butterflies. There are coconuts and mango farms, an orchid plantation and botanical gardens. Ethnic custom performance and an elephant show are held every morning and afternoon here.

A theme park, Mini Siam is also a favorite place near Pattaya. It has scale models of important historical sites and temples in Thailand. There are the Temple of the Emerald Buddha, the Bridge over the River Kwai, Wat Arun, and more than 80 other miniatures relating to Thai history, and there are also a number of replications of landmarks from other countries, including the Eiffel Tower, Big Ben, and the Statue of Liberty.

Phuket

Phuket, 862 km distance from Bangkok, is the largest island in Thailand, and is about the size of Singapore. It is the major tourist attraction of Thailand. The surrounding waters contain much varied marine life, and the town is notable for its Sino-Portuguese architecture. It is a very attractive island for sightseeing, with lovely seashores and forested hillside. It is well known as the site of Patong Beach, a popular tropical beach resort.

Phuket's restaurants are excellent, and there are still plenty of beaches for snorkeling and other water sports. There is also a wide variety of nonbeach activities: Tours of coconut and rubber plantations, Buddhist temples, batik factories, a cultured-pearl farm, a crocodile farm, the Marine Biological Research Center, a number of parks and the nearby islands off Rawai Beach are possibilities. To get around, consider renting a jeep or motorcycle, or flag down one of the songthaews (trucks that serve as buses) that constantly ply the route. If you're visiting between November and February, you can watch giant sea turtles going ashore to lay eggs on Mai Khao Beach.

Chiang Mai

Chiang Mai, the Rose of the North, is located in the region where much of the world's opium is grown. It is the nation's second largest city and has most of Bangkok's amenities including excellent food and accommodations. It was once the capital of an independent kingdom and the moat around the original town is still intact. Handicrafts of silk, silver and wood are timeless souvenirs for visitors from all over the world. Along with all this, a wide variety of accommodations, restaurants and entertainment all help to make Chiang Mai, one of Thailand's prime tourist attractions. Chiang Mai is also the land of magnificent temples and beautiful nature sites. Temples of interest here are Wat Chedi Luang, Wat Chiang Man, Wat Ku Tao and others. Trekking, hiking and nature tours are other activities popular in the regions of Chiang Mai.

The city's sights can be seen in a day, but most people use the town as a jumping-off point for exploring the region. Several hill tribes live in the area, and trekkers can visit tribal villages. If you aren't taking a trek, visit the night market to watch the local hill tribe members buying and selling. If you're looking for a day trip, go see the elephants being trained at the Elephant Conservation Center near Lampang. This village also has interesting blue and white pottery and an old fortress temple, Wat Lampang Luang.

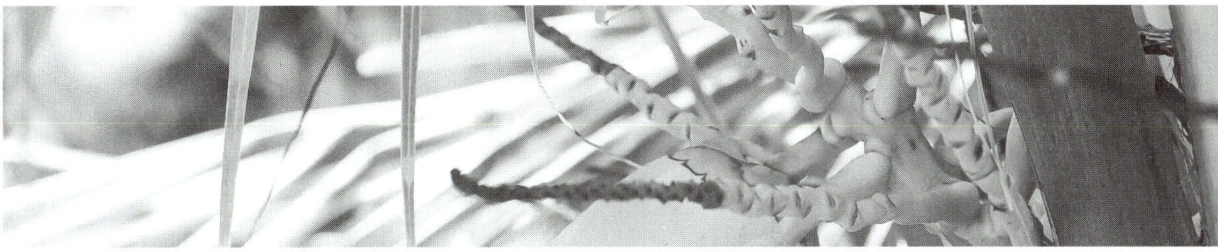

CHAPTER 3

Malaysia

Malaysia, Truly Asia | Unit 1

Vocabulary & Grammar Practice

[1] Which of the following best completes the sentences?

There are 8,000 (   ) of flowering plants in Peninsular Malaysia alone, including 2,000 tree species, 800 different orchids and 200 types of palm.

a) species

b) bunches

c) collection

d) community

[2] Unscramble the words to find the correct definitions for the words below.

a) tip: something, of, the end

➜

b) strait: that, two seas, a narrow passage of water, links

➜

c) merge: one thing, together, to form, join

➜

d) crossroad: where, place, two roads, meet

➜

e) carve: wood or stone, a shape, to cut, into

➜

f) skewer: a piece of food, a hole, to make, through

➜

g) concoction: a drink, different things, mixing, made, by

➜

h) stall: an open front, a small shop, with

➜

i) lamb: the flesh, lamb or sheep, of

➜

j) utensil: a tool, in cooking, with a particular use

➜

[3] **Match each word in the first column with its meaning in the second column.**

a) tip •	• a) the pointed end of something
b) strait •	• b) become one
c) merge •	• c) having control or authority
d) dominant •	• d) a narrow passage of water connecting two seas
e) tongue •	• e) language; movable organ in the mouth, used in talking, tasting, etc.
f) evolution •	• f) existing or spreading everywhere
g) confine •	• g) method
h) pervasive •	• h) all the animals living in a particular area
i) means •	• i) keep within limit
j) fauna •	• j) the gradual change and development of an idea, situation, or object

Reading or Listening Practice

[1] Think about the following questions.

1. Name the countries around Malaysia.

   ____

2. Name the different peoples that make up Malaysia's population.

   ____

3. What is the major religion in Malaysia?

   ____

4. What is the major language in Malaysia?

   ____

5. Name the tourist attractions in Malaysia.

   ____

[2] Read or listen to the following passages and answer the above questions.

Truly Asia

Malaysia, located in the heart of Southeast Asia, is divided into two main regions: Peninsular Malaysia, which lies just south of Thailand, and East Malaysia, which can be found north of Indonesia on the island of Borneo. Geographically, it is the southernmost tip of the Asian mainland. Further South is Singapore, across the Straits of Johor. But there is more Malaysia eastwards beyond the South China Sea where the states of Sarawak and Sabah are located. Both these states are part of the world's third largest island – Borneo. Because of its central location, between the Indian Ocean and the South China Sea, Malaysia has traditionally been a meeting point for traders and travelers from both the East and West.

Malaysia, formed in 1963 through a merging of the former British colonies of Malaya and Singapore, is a multicultural society, with Malays, Chinese and Indians living side by side. The Malays are the largest community. They are Muslims, speak Bahasa and are largely responsible for the political fortunes of the country. The Chinese comprise about a third of the population. They are Buddhists and Taoists, speak Hokkein, Hakka and Cantonese and are dominant in the business community. The Indians account for about 10% of the population. They are mainly Hindu Tamis and they speak Tamil, Malayalam, and some Hindi, and live mainly in the larger towns on the west coast of the peninsula. Eurasians and indigenous tribes make up the remaining population.

Malaysia's national language is Bahasa Melayu (Malay language). Although Bahasa Melayu is the official language, the mother tongues of the other communities such as Hokkien, Hakka, Tamil, Mandarin, Bennggali and others are also widely spoken. On top of this is a wide range of dialects representing the various sub roots of the races themselves. The evolution of Manglish (Malaysian English) has taken a life of its own. It is not only confined to the use of the suffix 'lah', but is more pervasive than can be imagined. In practice, you'll be able to get by with English in almost all the areas in the country, since the language is often used as a means of communication between the races, as well as being the language of business.

The weather in Malaysia is tropical without extremely high temperatures. Days are very warm, while nights are fairly cool. Average temperature is between 21 to 32 degree Celsius. Humidity is high. Rain tends to occur between November to February on the east coast of Peninsular Malaysia, on western Sarawak, and north-eastern Sabah. On the west coast of Peninsular Malaysia the rainy seasons are April to May and October to November.

There are 8,000 species of flowering plants in Peninsular Malaysia alone, including 2,000 tree species, 800 different orchids and 200 types of palm. Fauna includes elephants, tigers, leopards, sun bears, orangutans and varied bird populations in the world. More than 60 percent of the country is still rainforest.

Malaysia is one of the most satisfying tourist destinations in the world. Popular destinations include Kuala Lumpur, Malacca, Johor Bahru, and so forth.

CHAPTER 3

Malaysia

Shopping & Food in Malaysia

Unit 2

Vocabulary & Grammar Practice

[1] Which of the following is closest to the meaning of the underlined word?

Because Malaysia is a country of diverse cultures and traditions, it is not surprising that its cuisine is just as diverse.

a) food b) economy

c) language d) religion

[2] Which of the following best completes the sentences?

Most meals are eaten by using your (   ), while eating utensils are kept to a minimum.

a) fingers b) chopsticks

c) knives d) spoons

[3] Match each word in the first column with its meaning in the second column.

a) crossroad •	• a) to have the most importance or influence
b) brocade •	• b) making or inscribing by cutting
c) pewter •	• c) decorative cloth usually of silk, often with a raised pattern of gold or silver threads
d) brass •	• d) place where two roads meet and cross each other
e) kite •	• e) gray alloy of tin with lead or other metal
f) carving •	• f) very hard bright yellow metal
g) household •	• g) to make a hole through a piece of food; an object with a skewer or with something similar
h) predominate •	• h) a young sheep; the meat of a young sheep
i) lamb •	• i) family; connected with looking after a house and the people in it
j) skewer •	• j) a wooden or metal frame covered with paper or cloth for flying in the air

Reading or Listening Practice

[1] Think about the following questions.

1. *List products that can be purchased in Malaysia.*

2. *Name foods you can enjoy in Malaysia.*

3. *Write the key points, based on what you heard (read) from the below passages.*

[2] Read or listen to the following passages and answer the above questions.

Malaysia Shopping & Dining

Malaysia is a shoppers' paradise. Since it is situated at the crossroads of Asia, it presents visitors the best that the region has to offer. Among the items high on the shopping list of tourists are batik, silverwork, gold and silver brocade, local handicrafts, kites, pewter, brassware and carvings. The variety of bargain items you can find in the major markets is endless, ranging from quality electronics to traditional arts and crafts. Kota Bharu is one of the best places to shop for handicrafts. Langkawi has duty-free areas with bargains on electronics, household goods and jewelry.

You could travel to Malaysia just to eat: The variety of food is incredible. Because Malaysia is a country of diverse cultures and traditions, it is not surprising that its cuisine is just as varied. Chinese, Indian and Malay cuisines predominate, though in restaurants in larger cities we've even had French and North African dishes.

Some traditional Malay dishes include rendang (beef, lamb and chicken in coconut milk), satay (skewered meat in peanut sauce), pulut (various sticky-rice concoctions cooked inside a banana leaf), ikan bilis (dried anchovies fried in a sauce and served with rice) and murtabak (crepes stuffed with egg, meat and vegetables). Chicken, fish, noodles and curries are everywhere. Rice is the staple diet in any Malay meal. The Malaysian food is spicy, and coconut milk is a common ingredient. Most meals are eaten by using your fingers, and eating utensils are kept to a minimum. All dishes are served at the same time, accompanied by a refreshing drink. Fish is popular in Malay cooking, as with other seafood such as shrimps and cuttlefish. Authentic Malay food is not as widely available in Malaysian restaurants as Chinese style or American fast food. Restaurants in large hotels offer international cuisine from such countries as Japan, Korea, France and Italy. The street stalls offer delicious and cheap Malaysian food. Malaysia also offers a cornucopia of delicious tropical fruit: rambutan (similar to lychee), mangosteen (probably the best-tasting tropical fruit) and the infamous durian (undoubtedly the world's smelliest).

English for Tourism
Tourist Information & Creative Thinking for Language Learners

CHAPTER 3

Malaysia

Tourist Attractions | Unit 3

Vocabulary Practice

Which word does the following definition refer to?

1. *a tower that is used for religious worship in Asia*

   a) pagoda b) causeway

   c) post d) attractions

2. *a creature that is hunted and killed for food by another animal*

   a) horse b) prey

   c) fauna d) flora

3. *luxurious and expensive*

   a) verdant b) exotic

   c) sumptuous d) invaluable

4. *delightful*

   a) delectable b) expensive

   c) focal d) crazy

5. *remote inland districts*

   a) causeway b) plain

   c) plateau d) outback

Speaking Practice

How do you say the following in English?

1. 말레이시아는 동남아시아의 심장부에 위치해 있다.

2. 동남아시아의 심장부에 위치해 있는 말레이시아는 다문화 사회이다.

3. 조호바루(Johor Bahru)는 말레이시아의 남쪽 끝에 자리하고 있다.

4. 말레이시아의 남쪽 끝에 위치한 Johor Bahru는 싱가포르와 방죽길로 연결되어 있다.

5. 페낭(Penang)은 오랫동안 동양의 진주로 알려져 오고 있다.

6. 동양의 진주로 알려진 Penang은 열대 섬 리조트이다.

7. 말라카(Malacca)에 있는 역사적 건물은 네덜란드인이 건축한 것이다.

8. 그 절에는 7층 석탑이 있다.

9. 중국인이 인구의 약 1/3을 차지한다.

10. 낮은 매우 따뜻한 반면 밤은 꽤 시원하다.

Reading or Listening Practice

Johor Bahru

Located at the southern tip of the Peninsula, Johor Bahru (JB) is the third largest state in Peninsular Malaysia. Connected to Singapore by road and rail via a modern causeway, JB is a popular destination for Singaporeans as well as visitors visiting the island republic.

JB, in short, was established in 1855 by the late Sultan Abu Bakar (the Father of Modern Johor) and now serves as the administrative and commercial center of the state. Consisting of a diverse ethnic mix of races, JB offers the visitor heritage attractions, colorful culture, delectable local cuisine, and exciting recreational activities.

Shopping opportunities abound in JB. Modern malls, arcades, handicraft centers, bazaars and markets offering international and local products all vie for attention. Local craftwork is sure to catch the eye and they do make lovely souvenirs of a trip here. Another interesting side of JB can be experienced when night falls over the city. A sumptuous array of food stalls and vendors appear.

Penang

Penang, the 'Pearl of the Orient' needs little introduction to many visitors to Malaysia, having long been known as one of Southeast Asia's finest destinations. It is a tropical island resort situated in the north-western tip of Peninsular Malaysia close to South Thailand. Penang's outstanding beaches and exotic sights have made it one of the most popular destinations in the region. The Kek Lok Si temple, at Air Itam, is reputed to be the most beautiful and largest temple complex in Southeast Asia. Its seven-story pagoda, over 90 feet high, is a harmonious blend of Chinese, Thai, and Burmese architecture and craftsmanship.

Other worthwhile stops are the delightful Penang Bird Park, the romantic peak of Penang Hill, and Fort Cornwallis. A journey through the reserve's interior reveals rare flora, monkeys chattering in the trees, sea eagles surveying their prey, and maybe a glimpse of a Hawksbill turtle heading for the sea. Some hotels organize early morning treks through the forest.

Sarawak

Lying on the northwest coast of Bornes, Sarawak is on the third largest island in the world. It is the largest state in Malaysia and an outback of sheer beauty rich in resources such as pepper, cocoa, palm oil timber and oil. With an area of 124,450 sq. km, it is a region of endless fascination, possessing the largest cave chamber in the world, verdant jungles, unique fauna and flora, white beaches, and remote islands. Its population of 1.5 million people is as rich and varied as the land.

Sarawak is also known as 'the land of many rivers.' The river provides means of transportation and communication. Like Sabah, Sarawak is known to international visitors primarily because of the extraordinary natural wonders of its national parks, including Gunung Mulu, the Niah Caves, and Bako.

The capital of Sarawak is Kuching. Malasia Airlines flies regularly to Kuching International Airport as well as to Miri from Kuala Lumpur, Johor Bahru, Singapore, and Kota Kinabalu. Boats are a common mode of transport in Sarawak. Travel, in areas no reachable by boat, is often by light aircrafts and helicopters. Major towns are serviced by buses.

Malacca

Malacca, located on the Western Coast of the Malaysian Peninsula, is the oldest town in Malaysia. It is an interesting blend of Chinese, Portuguese, Dutch and

British influences and is considered Malaysia's most historic city.

The town, an important trading post in the fourteenth century, was ruled by the Portuguese in the sixteenth century and was then conquered by the Dutch in 1644. The center of Malacca is fairly small and easy to walk around in a day. Many of the historic buildings in Malacca were built by the Dutch or Portuguese. Around the town center the attractions include the Stadhuys, Christ Church and St. Francis Xavier's Church. And the city remains full of intriguing Chinese streets, antique shops, temples and nostalgic reminders of the European colonial powers. Sloping rooftops of traditional Malay houses still hang over the water, and seem to call out sleepily from the past. The river side is a part of the city that seems to have defied the Portuguese, who captured the city in 1511 and occupied it for over a century.

CHAPTER 4

Indonesia

Unit 1 Indonesia, the Lonely Planet

Vocabulary & Grammar Practice

[1] Which of the following is closest to the meaning of the underlined word?

Indonesia is the largest country in Southeast Asia, the largest group of islands in the world, and is best known for its numerous island resorts peppered across the archipelago.

a) land
b) continent
c) archipelago
d) ocean

[2] Unscramble the words to find the correct definitions for the words below.

a) peak: sharply, pointed, mountain, top, a

➜

b) leather: animal, skin, shoes, bags, etc., used, treated, making, for

➜

c) archipelago: many, islands, of, group

➜

d) encompass: all, sides, surround, on, to

➜

e) landscape: country, scenery, a, view, wide, of

➜

f) migrate: to move, to, from, one place, another

➜

g) mosque: Muslims, worship, a building, in, which

➜

h) plantation: crops, grown, land, piece, of, a large, are, where

➜

i) monsoon: India and neighboring countries, the heavy rains, fall, in, which

➜

j) deter: acting, from, prevent, to

➜

[3] **Match each word in the first column with its meaning in the second column.**

a) archipelago •	• a) group of many islands
b) numerous •	• b) to stretch over
c) encompass •	• c) very many
d) span •	• d) to surround on all sides
e) roughly •	• e) equal in value, amount, meaning
f) equivalent •	• f) thick
g) landscape •	• g) about, more or less
h) lush •	• h) a tree of tropical countries which grows on muddy land and near water
i) peak •	• i) a sharply pointed mountain top
j) mangrove •	• j) a wide view of country scenery

Reading or Listening Practice

[1] Think about the following questions.

1. Name the countries around Indonesia.

   ____

2. Which months are best for sightseeing in Indonesia?

   ____

3. Name the peoples that make up Indonesia's population.

   ____

4. What is the major language in Indonesia?

   ____

5. What is the major religion in Indonesia?

   ____

[2] Read or listen to the following passages and answer the above questions.

Indonesia, the Lonely Planet

Indonesia is the largest country in Southeast Asia, the largest archipelago in the world, and is best known for its numerous island resorts peppered across the archipelago. Of these, Bali, Lombok and Bintan are the most popular. Encompassing a large area between Australia and Asia, Indonesia is New Zealand's closest Asian neighbour. The Indonesian archipelago, comprising more than 13,000 islands, shares borders with Malaysia and Papua New Guinea and sea border with Singapore, Thailand, Vietnam, the Philippines and Australia.

The name Indonesia has its roots in two Greek words : "Indos" meaning Indian and "Nesos" which means islands. Indonesia's natural landscape ranges from rain forest and lush grasslands, to volcanic peaks and semi-desert. Under 10 percent of the total land area is suitable for farming, while two-thirds consists of woodland, forests and mangrove swamp. The main islands include Java, Sumatra, Sulawesi, Bali, Kalimantan, Nusa Tenggara, Maluku, and Irian Jaya.

Because Indonesia is situated around the equator the climate is tropical, hot and humid and is more moderate in the highlands. The eastern monsoon from June to September brings dry weather while the western monsoon from December to March brings moisture-laden rain. The transitional period between these two are interposed by occasional rain showers, but even in the midst of the western monsoon season, temperatures range from 21℃ (70°F) to 33℃ (90°F) except at higher altitudes which are much cooler. Heaviest rainfalls are recorded in December and January. Humidity is between 60 and 100 percent. Though travel in the wet season is possible in most parts of Indonesia, it can be a deterrent to some activities and travel on mud-clogged roads in less developed areas is difficult. In general, the best time to visit is in the dry season between May and October.

There are a lot of ethnic divisions in Indonesia mostly split up by the separated islands but due to migration projects the ethnic groups are found all over the nation. From the total population 45% are Javanese, 14% are Sundanese, 7.5% are Madurese, 7.5% are coastal Malays and 26% belong to other ethnic groups.

Due to the multi-ethnic divisions, over 300 languages are spoken in the archipelago and most belong to the Malay-Polynesian group. Within this group, many regional languages and dialects are spoken. On the island of Alor alone there are about 70 dialects and on Sulawesi 62 languages were identified. Still to be explored is Irian Jaya where till now more than 300 languages were found. Some languages are spoken only by two people and are as good as died out. Several scientists are now searching for unknown languages in order to register them and trying to get anything of it on paper. Bahassa Indonesia or Indonesian is the official national language now. In all tourist destination areas English is the number one foreign language fairly spoken and written, whereas some Dutch is still spoken and understood in the bigger cities and French increasing in its popularity at the better hotels and restaurants.

The majority of the population (about 85%) are Moslems, ten percent are Christians, two percent are Hindus, and three percent are either Buddhists or animists. However, Churches, Hindu and Buddhist temples are found throughout the country, as are mosques of the Moslem faith.

CHAPTER 4

Indonesia

Shopping & Food in Indonesia

Unit 2

Vocabulary & Grammar Practice

[1] Which of the following is closest to the meaning of the underlined word?

Bargaining is customary in small shops and markets, the art of which is to start at half the asking price and slowly increase your offer until a settlement is reached.

a) compromise

b) comprehension

c) conflict

d) decision

[2] Which of the following best completes the sentences?

Other craft forms include ikat, (   ) is a type of weaving with tie-dyed threads.

a) that

b) who

c) which

d) what

[3] Match each word in the first column with its meaning in the second column.

a) leather •	• a) treated animal skin used for making shoes, bags, etc.
b) apply •	• b) a solid material made out of fats or oils used to make candles
c) wax •	• c) to walk slowly for pleasure
d) customary •	• d) having a pleasant or acceptable taste
e) compromise •	• e) to lay one thing on or in another; to ask for employment, acceptance, or admission
f) stroll •	• f) usual, habitual
g) flock •	• g) the act of settling an argument by each side taking a middle course acceptable to all sides
h) palatable •	• h) a large piece of land, esp. in hot countries, on which crops such as tea, sugar, and rubber are grown
i) seasonal •	• i) happening or active at a particular season
j) plantation •	• j) a group of sheep, goats, or birds; a crowd; to gather in large crowds

Reading or Listening Practice

[1] **Think about the following questions.**

1. *List products that can be purchased in Indonesia.*

2. *Name foods you can enjoy in Indonesia.*

3. *Write the key points, based on what you heard (read) from the below passages.*

[2] Read or listen to the following passages and answer the above questions.

Indonesia Shopping & Dining

Indonesia is one of the world's shopping paradises. You can shop for batiks, silver, cloth, porcelain, wood and leather goods. The exact list is varied by location. Batik, the art of applying wax to cloth and the tie-dying in colorful and dramatic designs is produced throughout Indonesia, and has become high fashion in recent years. Other craft forms include ikat, which is a type of weaving with tie-dyed threads; songket, a silk cloth with gold or silver threads woven into it; and kris, artwork often decorated with jewels.

Today shops are available at a large variety of shopping centers and malls, providing international shopping environment with something to excite the whole family. A quick stroll through the city's main shopping centers at Plaza Indonesia, Plaza Senayan, Sarinah, Pasar Roya, Blok M Plaza and Mal Pondok Indah will send heads spinning with an amazing variety of the world famous brands available. People are now flocking to Indonesia to shop for very good reasons.

For most Indonesian people, a meal consists of steamed white rice with side dishes of meat, chicken, fish and vegetables along with a glass of tea. However, each province or area has its own cuisine, which varies in the method of cooking and ingredients. The Japanese cuisine is probably more palatable to the general taste and consists of vegetables, soybeans, beef, chicken and other varieties. The Sumatrans generally eat more beef compared to the other regions. In Bali, Irian Jaya and the highlands of North Sumatra and North Sulawesi pork dishes are specialities. As the population of Indonesia is predominantly Moslem, pork is usually not served except in Chinese restaurants, non-Moslem regions and in places serving international cuisine. Chinese restaurants are found all over the country. There are also fine restaurants specializing in Continental,

Japanese and Korean cuisine. There is such a rich variety in the Indonesian cuisine that one should sample specialities in each area. However, most common nationwide are "sate" (skewered grilled meat), "gado-gado" (vegetables salad with a peanut sauce), "nasi goreng" (fried rice served at anytime) and "bakmi goreng" (fried noodles).

There is also a wide variety of tropical and sub-tropical vegetables all year round. Fruit is available throughout the year. Some fruits such as mangoes and water melons are seasonal, but most of the other fruits can be bought throughout the whole year, such as bananas, apples, papayas, pineapples, oranges, etc. Coffee and tea plantations are plentiful, growing on several islands, and served everywhere from fine restaurants to small village stalls.

English for Tourism

Tourist Information & Creative Thinking for Language Learners

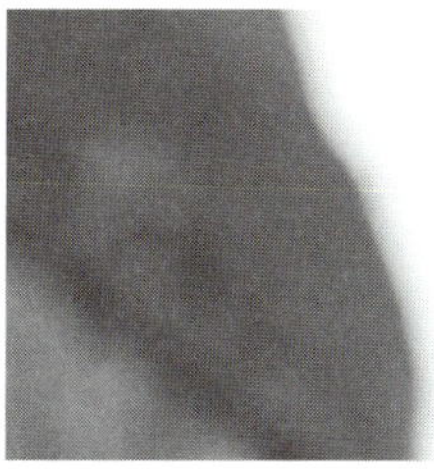

CHAPTER 4

Indonesia

Tourist Attractions | Unit 3

Vocabulary Practice

Which word does the following definition refer to?

1. *to supply land or crops with water*

a) irrigate
b) retain
c) cultivate
d) harvest

2. *very strict*

a) sacred
b) rigid
c) gentle
d) flexible

3. *native*

a) natural
b) luxurious
c) indigenous
d) simple

4. *all the plants of a particular place or country*

a) fauna
b) flora
c) botanical
d) plantation

5. *a tube that allows a swimmer to breathe air under water*

a) wax
b) boat
c) telescope
d) snorkel

Speaking Practice

How do you say the following in English?

1. 인도네시아는 세계에서 가장 큰 군도이다.

2. 세계에서 가장 큰 군도인 인도네시아는 동남아시아에서 가장 큰 나라이다.

3. 인도네시아의 인구는 압도적으로 회교도이다.

4. 중국 음식점을 전역에 볼 수 있다.

5. Bali는 힌두교에 기반을 두고 있다.

6. 인도네시아는 적도 부근에 위치해 있다.

7. 그는 TV를 보면서 항상 식사를 한다.

8. 그녀는 나에게 미소를 지으면서 나와 악수를 하였다.

9. 길을 따라 걷다가 그녀를 만났다.

10. 방문객의 수와 발맞추어 더 많은 호텔을 짓고 있습니다.

Reading or Listening Practice

Bali

The island of Bali is mountainous in the center with a cluster of volcanoes of which one is the active Mount Agung and considered sacred. Terraced rice-fields dominate the landscape, with small streams bringing water for irrigation.

Bali's culture is based on its unique form of Hinduism which has been retained after the Islamization of Java. Though the caste system is observed, it is not as rigid as in India. Religion is the source of traditional customs in family and community life. Its influence is also strongly felt in the arts. With a completely different lifestyle from the rest of Indonesia, the Balinese have managed to preserve their culture despite the overwhelming foreign influences brought by the increasing number of visitors. A friendly people, the Balinese who are more exposed to international tourists, generally speak more English than people in other parts of Indonesia. Keeping pace with the number of visitors and the need for their accommodations, more hotels have been built, from small bungalow types for the budget traveler to the luxurious Nusa Dua tourist resort area. Water sports have gained in popularity: surfing on Kuta, wind surfing at Sanur, sailing and scuba diving at several other tourist parts.

Irian Jaya

Irian Jaya is a land of exceptional natural grandeur. Its jungles are among the wildest, most impenetrable in the world. It has scenic beaches in abundance as well as immense stretches of marshlands. Cool grassy meadows lie at the foot of the towering mountains. The highest peak of the central mountain range is Puncak Jayawijaya (5,500 meters). Second and third are Gunung Trikora (5,160 meters) and Gunung Yamin (5,100 meters), respectively. The biggest lake is Paniai.

On the basis of physical features and differences in language, customs, artistic expression and other aspects of culture, the indigenous people of Irian Jaya are distinguished into about 250 sub-groups, although they all belong to the Melanesian race, and are related to the people inhabiting the islands along the southern rim of the Pacific. The Negritos are believed to have settled on the island first, probably some 3,000 years ago, followed by the Melanesians. The people of the central highlands still maintain their ancestral customs and traditions, and are virtually untouched by alien influences.

Jakarta

Jakarta, the nation's capital, started as a small harbor town, Sunda Kelapa, but its founding dates back to 1,570 when it was named Jayakarta (City of Great Victory) by Fatahillah of the neighboring Sultanate of Banten. The name was later changed to Batavia under the Dutch. Now a center of government, business and industry, the city spreads over an area of 656 sq. km (410 sq. miles) and has a population of over seven million.

The main gateway to Indonesia, Jakarta is a contrast of modern western architecture and traditional Indonesian culture. Its rapid growth into a metropolitan city reflects the economic, political, social and industrial development of the nation. In recent years, Jakarta has expanded its facilities for the visitor with luxury hotels, fine restaurants, exciting night-life and shopping centers besides tourist attractions like "Beautiful Indonesia in Miniature" Park, restored colonial period buildings, sea resorts in the Bay of Jakarta, and an extensive beach recreation complex.

Sulawesi

Sulawesi has become a very popular tourist destination. It offers beautiful flora and fauna and is home to many different ethnic groups. Sulawesi's dive sites are among the most spectacular in the world. Sulawesi is also excellent for snorkelers. Many dive schools operate in Sulawesi. Dive schools also offer snorkeling trips, however it is perhaps more suitable for the snorkelers to arrange their own boat trips as dive schools often cater only to the requirements of divers and snokelers may end up visiting sites that are not very exciting for them. Sulawesi can be very easily reached by air, either from other parts of Indonesia or from Singapore.

CHAPTER 5

Singapore

Unit 1 Singapore, the Garden City of Asia

Vocabulary & Grammar Practice

[1] Which of the following best completes the sentences?

It joined Malaysia in 1963, but withdrew two years later and became (   ).

a) dependent
b) independent
c) merged
d) inhibited

[2] Unscramble the words to find the correct definitions for the words below.

a) withdraw: away or back, to move
→

b) uninhibited: action and behavior, in, free
→

c) souvenir: an event, trip, place, etc., of, a reminder, as, kept, an object
→

d) artifact: human beings, by, produced or shaped, an object
→

e) curio: because it is old, beautiful, or rare, object, small, that is valuable
→

f) suburbs: an area, a lot of people, the center of a town or city, where, away from, live
→

g) outlet: a store, a particular manufacturer or wholesaler, the goods, that, of, sells
→

h) retailer: someone, things, who, a shop, in, sells
→

i) counter offer: offer made, somebody else, in reply to, an offer made by
→

j) fragrant: a, smell, pleasant, having
→

[3] Match each word in the first column with its meaning in the second column.

a) stable •	• a) great number
b) withdraw •	• b) to convert to a religion
c) uninhibited •	• c) free in action and behavior
d) barely •	• d) consequence
e) visible •	• e) of or suitable for ordinary, informal, or familiar conversation
f) apparent •	• f) obvious
g) colloquial •	• g) noticeable to the eye
h) outcome •	• h) only just, hardly
i) proselytize •	• i) to move away or back
j) multitude •	• j) not easily upset

Reading or Listening Practice

[1] Think about the following questions.

1. Name the countries around Singapore.

   ____

2. Which months are best for sightseeing in Singapore?

   ____

3. Name the different peoples that make up Singapore's population.

   ____

4. What is the major language in Singapore?

   ____

5. What is the major religion in Singapore?

   ____

[2] Read or listen to the following passages and answer the above questions.

Singapore, the Garden City of Asia

Founded as a British trading colony in 1819, Singapore consists of the main island of Singapore and more than 50 smaller islands. It is a small, stable, and highly developed island country. It joined Malaysia in 1963, but withdrew two years later and became independent. About half of the smaller islands of Singapore are uninhibited. Some of the islands have been developed for recreation and tourism.

Singapore is shaped almost like a diamond. It is located at the southern tip of the Malay Peninsular, connected by a 1-kilometer-long causeway. Singapore's immediate neighbors are Malaysia, Brunei, Darussalam and Indonesia. Being very close to the equator, Singapore's climate is characterized by abundant rainfall, relatively uniform temperature and high humidity throughout the year. Singapore's temperature rarely drops below 20 degrees Celsius during the day making it hot and humid all year round. Singapore is wettest from November to January and is driest from May to July. The difference between the two is barely visible. June and August are claimed to be the best time to visit, but even then it rains often. When it dose rain, it's generally only for a short period every day. Light summer clothing should be worn.

Singapore is a multi-cultural city. Diversity is the key to Singapore's population: Chinese, Malay, Indonesia and others. Although citizens of all races think of themselves as Singaporean, there are still certain areas that are inhabited by specific ethnic groups. Each area has its own culture celebrating its own religion. Due to many ethnic groups, Singapore has a dazzling range of languages. The official languages in Singapore are Malay, Chinese (Mandarin), Tamil and English. Malay is the national language and English is the language of administration and business. It is extremely rare for a person to be monolingual - most people are bilingual from infancy and it is common for people to know and use four or five languages in their daily life. Naturally the presence of other languages has influenced the English of Singapore. The influence is especially apparent in the kind of English that is used informally, which is popularly called Singlish. As most Singaporeans use a lot of Singaporean colloquial English to their children, children tend to speak Singaporean colloquial English.

The diversity of religions existed in Singapore is an outcome of various nationalities residing there. More than half of the Singapore's population are the followers of Buddhism and Taoism. The statistical fact about Singapore indicates that Chinese people are the largest ethnic group in Singapore, so there leaves no doubt why they are Buddhists or Taoists as these two religions were originally brought with them from China. But later some of them proselytized to Christianity influenced by the arrival of the Raffles. Most of Singapore's Indians are Hindus, though some of them are Muslims.

Tourism in Singapore offers you a multitude of tourist activities. There are destinations as diverse as marine parks, zoo gardens, museums and the famous Sentosa as well as the Singapore Isles.

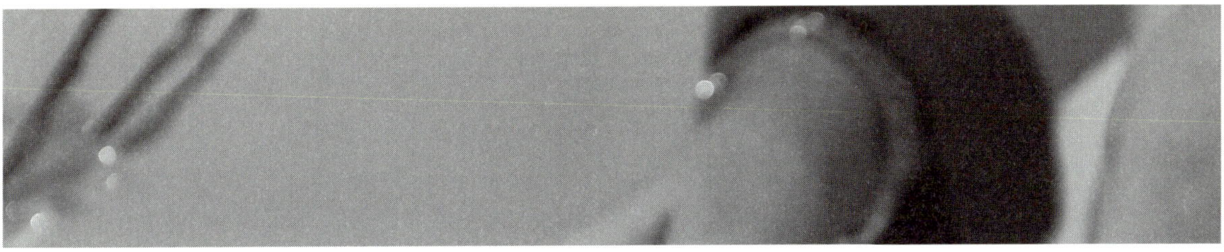

CHAPTER 5

Singapore

Shopping & Food in Singapore

Unit 2

Vocabulary & Grammar Practice

[1] Which of the following is closest to the meaning of the underlined word?

<u>Fixed</u> prices are the rule at department stores and at an increasing number of other outlets.

a) Set
b) Cheap
c) Bargaining
d) Expensive

[2] Which of the following best completes the sentences?

When bargaining in a flexible-price store, begin by asking the retailer for his 'best price' and then make your (   ) offer.

a) nice
b) counter
c) active
d) low

[3] Match each word in the first column with its meaning in the second column.

a) souvenir •	• a) small object that is valuable because it is old, beautiful, or rare
b) artifact •	• b) an area away from the center of a town or city, where a lot of people live
c) curio •	• c) someone who sells things in a shop
d) suburbs •	• d) an object produced or shaped by human beings
e) ambience •	• e) having a pleasant smell
f) outlet •	• f) an object kept as a reminder of an event, trip, place etc.
g) retailer •	• g) offer made in reply to an offer made by somebody else
h) counter offer •	• h) environment; atmosphere
i) fragrant •	• i) grill
j) broil •	• j) a store that sells the goods of a particular manufacturer or wholesaler

Reading or Listening Practice

[1] Think about the following questions.

1. *List products that can be purchased in Singapore.*

2. *Name foods you can enjoy in Singapore.*

3. *Write the key points, based on what you heard (read) from the below passages.*

[2] Read or listen to the following passages and answer the above questions.

Singapore Shopping & Dining

Singapore may be one of the smallest countries in size, but it is big on shopping. Souvenirs of Singapore can be found all over town in major department stores, shops and hotel shopping arcades. They range from T-shirts to local handicraft items. Health-giving ginseng can be found at Chinese medical halls all over Singapore. The city is also an international marketplace of jewelry, sporting goods, fashions, watches, cameras, electronics, Asian artifacts and curios. The best time to shop is during the six-week "Great Singapore Sale" from late May to early July, when almost all the shops in town offer good discounts. The most internationally famous shopping district in Singapore is the Orchard Road shopping belt, with major shopping centers such as Counterpoint and the Heeren. If you venture out to the suburbs, the prices will be cheaper and the ambience less touristy.

Fixed prices are the rule at department stores and at an increasing number of other outlets. Bargaining is mostly confined to smaller stores. When bargaining in a flexible-price store, begin by asking the retailer for his 'best price' and then make your counter offer. Once you agree on a price with the shopkeeper, you are expected not to back out, so don't be hasty and make an offer unless you are serious about buying. Generally you can expect to save from 10%~30% through bargaining.

The food of Singapore reflects its multiethnic society. Almost every major international cuisine can be found in Singapore, with hundreds of restaurants dotted around the island. Chinese contributes to 10 percent of the population in Singapore, hence Chinese cuisine is one of the most popular cuisine in Singapore. Indian and Malayan dishes are also available. Chinese dishes include Char Kewy Teow (fried noodles), Popiah (fresh spring rolls) and Chicken Rice while Malay dishes include Nasi Lemak (fragrant rice in coconut milk) and Satay (skewered meat broiled over red-hot coals and dipped in peanut sauce).

English for Tourism
Tourist Information & Creative Thinking for Language Learners

CHAPTER 5

Singapore

Tourist Attractions | Unit 3

Vocabulary Practice

1. *a table or a small shop with an open front, especially outdoors, where goods are sold*

   a) stall　　b) retail

   c) plate　　d) arcade

2. *a piece of jewellery or a small pretty object that is not worth much money*

   a) trinket　　b) flea market

   c) article　　d) item

3. *a large cage where birds are kept*

   a) coop　　b) fence

   c) aviary　　d) compartment

4. *to walk somewhere in a slow relaxed way*

   a) haste　　b) stroll

   c) skip　　d) jump

5. *capable of transmitting light so that object or image can be seen*

   a) emplacement　　b) transparent

   c) barrier　　d) nocturnal

Speaking Practice

How do you say the following in English?

1. 규칙적으로 운동하는 것이 중요하다.

2. 싱가포르에서는 사람들이 4개 언어를 사용하는 것이 흔하다.

3. 클락키(Clarke Quay)는 싱가포르의 유일한 강가 마을이다.

4. Clarke Quay는 식사, 쇼핑, 그리고 오락을 결합하고 있는 싱가포르의 유일한 강가 마을이다.

5. Clarke Quay는 주지사인 Clarke의 이름을 따서 지어졌다.

6. 싱가포르의 주지사인 Clarke의 이름을 딴 Clarke는 상업의 중심시였다.

7. 센토사(Sentosa) 섬은 싱가포르의 거대한 테마공원이다.

8. Sentosa 섬은 매년 수많은 방문객을 끌어 들이는 싱가포르의 거대한 테마공원이다.

9. Underwater World는 아시아의 가장 흥미 있는 열대 수족관으로 칭송 받고 있다.

10. 아시아의 가장 흥미 있는 열대 수족관으로 칭송받고 있는 Underwater World에는 80 미터의 투명한 터널이 있다.

Reading or Listening Practice

Clarke Quay

Clarke Quay is Singapore's only riverside village combining dining, shopping, and entertainment. Named after Singapore's second governor, Sir Andrew Clarke, Clarke Quay was the center of commerce in the late 19th century due to its strategic location near the mouth of Singapore River. On the 23,000 square meter site are fiver blocks of go-downs (warehouses) and shops, restored to their original 19th century style. These contain a spread of specialty restaurants, themed pubs and wine bars, and pedestrianized streets.

On weekends, Clarke Quay has a decent flea market with more than 100 stalls that sell a wide variety of antiques, trinkets and toys. The Clarke Quay Sunday Flea Mart is held every Sunday and it is a regular event which both locals and tourists can look forward to. The bustling flea mart adds color and flavor in the ambience of the Clarke Quay, where street activities and street life are abundant. Visitors can bargain their way through the 100 stalls selling a wide range of antiques, collections and handicrafts. Besides, you can enjoy the boat tour down the Singapore River, most popular with both the tourists and locals alike.

Jurong Bird Park

Southeast Asia's largest bird park, Jurong Bird Park is on the west of the island. Its collection of more than 8,000 birds from 600 species is among the largest in the world. Highlights include the world's largest collection of Southeast Asian Hornbills and South American Toucans, and the world's second largest penguin exhibit.

Most of the birds fly around in unfettered aviaries rather than small cages. You can stroll through a tropical rain forest and pass beneath one of the world's tallest, cascading waterfalls. The Parrot Paradise displays more than 500 parrots.

Sentosa

Sentosa Island, which is hugely popular with both locals and tourists alike, is Singapore's mega theme-park on an island. Attracting over three and a half million visitors each year, it is Singapore's most popular attraction. The island has a wide variety of museums, South-East Asia's largest oceanarium, a nineteenth century British fort complete with bunkers, tunnels and gun emplacements, a butterfly park and an insectarium. The offshore island of Sentosa, once the domain of tropical forest and rocky coasts, has been redeveloped into a sprawling amusement park where you can swim, sunbathe, visit a butterfly park and a wax museum. Sentosa offers a host of attractions for the whole family.

Underwater World, probably the most popular attraction on the island, draws huge crowds every day. Praised as Asia's most exciting tropical oceanarium, it has an 80-meter transparent tunnel which allows you to view over 2,500 sea creatures in close proximity. You can get the impression of having stepped under water, deep into the ocean. It can be reached by air, land or sea. Cable-cars and ferries run from the World Trade Center to this former military base half a kilometer offshore.

Singapore Zoological Gardens

Located beside the Mandai Orchid Gardens, Singapore Zoological Gardens is among the most beautiful zoos in Asia. It is a model of the 'open zoo' concept. Natural barriers instead of iron cages contain the animals. The zoo houses 2,800 animals of 216 species, from polar bears to regional fauna. The most famous animal of the Singapore Zoo is Ah, Meng, the Orang-Utan. This grand dame is the mascot of the zoo. Ah Meng poses for photos (with an attendant's help) having lunch or tea with zoo visitors.

One other significant feature of the zoo is the Night Safari, where visitors can view wild life at night, through special lighting techniques. The zoo's night safari is a chance to see 1,200 nocturnal animals from more than 100 species.

Indeed there is a plethora of things to do at the Singapore Zoo. They go there not just to see the animals but also to take in the scenic surroundings, taste the marvelous food available at the many restaurants or simply to have picnics. To add to its attraction, the zoo also has two exceptional Children's Playgrounds.

CHAPTER 6

Philippines, the Pearl of the Orient Seas

Unit 1

Vocabulary & Grammar Practice

[1] Which of the following is closest to the meaning of the underlined word?

The 7000 islands that <u>consist of</u> the Philippines are the forgotten islands of South-East Asia.

a) comprehend
b) inhabit
c) immigrate
d) comprise

[2] Unscramble the words to find the correct definitions for the words below.

a) Filipino: the Philippines, of, a native or inhabitant

➜

b) Pilipino: language, the Filipino

➜

c) considerable: amount, size, or degree, in, fairly, large

➜

d) statue: wood, stone, bronze, etc., in, a person, animal, etc., of, figure

➜

e) occupy: to, a country, of, possession, take

➜

f) peel: the skin, off, to take

➜

g) profess: a religious order, of, the vows, to take

➜

h) cloth: material, weaving, by, formed

➜

i) instruction: teaching, of, the act or action

➜

j) traverse: across, pass

➜

[3] Match each word in the first column with its meaning in the second column.

a) Filipino •	• a) to take possession of (a country or a site)
b) cede •	• b) to relinquish, yield
c) occupy •	• c) to take the vows of a religious order
d) unadulterated •	• d) to join or act together
e) traverse •	• e) the act or action of teaching
f) profess •	• f) the Filipino language
g) conspire •	• g) fairly large in amount, size, or degree
h) Pilipino •	• h) pure
i) considerable •	• i) pass across
j) instruction •	• j) a native or inhabitant of the Philippines

Reading or Listening Practice

[1] **Think about the following questions.**

1. Name the countries around the Philippines.

____

2. Which months are best for sightseeing in the Philippines?

____

3. Name the different peoples that make up the Philippines's population.

____

4. What is the major religion in the Philippines?

____

5. What is the major language in the Philippines?

____

[2] **Read or listen to the following passages and answer the above questions.**

Philippines, the Pearl of the Orient Seas

The Republic of the Philippines is an archipelago of 7,100 islands strategically situated in the Asia Pacific. It stands at the crossroads of the developed western world and the Orient. Taiwan, China and Hong Kong are northern neighbors and further north is Japan. To the west lie Southeast Asian countries such as Singapore, Malaysia and Thailand. Its three main islands are Luzon, Visayas and Mindanao. The 7,000 islands that comprise the Philippines are the forgotten islands of South-East Asia.

It has a rich history combining Asian, European, and American influences. Prior to Spanish colonization in 1521, the Filipinos had a rich culture and were trading with the Chinese and the Japanese. The Philippines were ceded by Spain to the US in 1898 following the Spanish-American War. They attained their independence in 1946 after being occupied by the Japanese in World War Ⅱ. In 1992, the US closed down its last military bases on the islands. Today, the Muslims, and some of the isolated tribes, are the only people whose culture remains unadulterated by Spanish and American influences.

The Philippines are chiefly of volcanic origin. Most of the larger islands are traversed by mountain ranges. Narrow coastal plains, wide valleys, volcanoes, dense forests, and mineral and hot springs further characterize the larger islands. Its total land area of almost 300,000 square kilometers includes mountain ranges, fertile coastal and central plains, rolling uplands and a coastline of 18,411 kilometers of which there are 60 natural harbors.

Its climate is generally tropical, with distinct seasons: the rainy season from June to September, cool and dry from October to February, and hot and mainly dry from March to May. Evenings are cooler. Typhoons occasionally occur from June to September. Average temperatures range from 24℃ to 31℃. The best time to visit is from November to March, when temperatures are cool and pleasant. April and May are very hot and humid. Avoid the rainy season from June to September, as roads are often damaged by flooding.

The great majority of the people of the Philippines belong to the Malay group and are known as Filipinos. Other groups include the Negritos (negroid pygmies) and the Dumagats (similar to the Papuans of New Guinea), and there is a small Chinese minority. The Filipinos constitute one of the largest Christian group in Asia. Roman Catholicism is professed by over 80% of the population and the rest are Protestants, the Philippine Independent Church.

The geography and history of the Philippines have conspired to produce a multiplicity of languages, some 80 dialects in total. The official national language is Pilipino. A considerable number of Filipinos speak English, the nation's second language. English is generally used for educational, governmental and commercial purposes and is widely understood since it is the medium of instruction in schools. The Philippines are the third largest group of English speaking people in the world, after the United States and the United Kingdom.

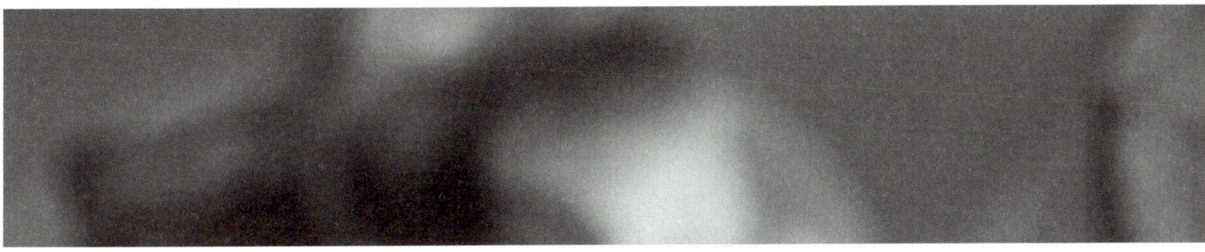

Philippines

CHAPTER 6

Shopping & Food in the Philippines

Unit 2

Vocabulary & Grammar Practice

[1] Which of the following is closest to the meaning of the underlined word?

World-famous Philippine furniture made from bamboo or exquisitely carved wood can be <u>priceless</u>.

a) cheap | b) trivial
c) resonable | d) very valuable

[2] Which of the following best completes the sentences?

The most obvious Chinese contribution is noodles, (   ) form the basis of the popular dishes.

a) that | b) who
c) what | d) which

[3] Match each word in the first column with its meaning in the second column.

a) statue •	• a) figure of a person, animal, etc. in wood, stone, bronze, etc.
b) icon •	• b) material formed by weaving or knitting natural or synthetic fibers
c) cloth •	• c) an idol
d) fiber •	• d) invaluable
e) priceless •	• e) a natural or synthetic filament, as of cotton or nylon
f) virtually •	• f) to explain
g) account for •	• g) to take the skin off
h) marinate •	• h) to soak (meat, for example) in a marinade
i) peel •	• i) cheap
j) inexpensive •	• j) in fact, nearly

Reading or Listening Practice

[1] **Think about the following questions.**

1. *List products that can be purchased in the Philippines.*

2. *Name foods you can enjoy in the Philippines.*

3. *Write the key points, based on what you heard (read) from the below passages.*

[2] Read or listen to the following passages and answer the above questions.

Philippine Shopping & Dining

Even the most seasoned shopper and bargain hunter would find shopping in the Philippines a delightful surprise. Anywhere a traveler might wander from the northernmost tip of Luzon to the southern bottom of Mindanao. Quality items can be bought for a bargain.

Philippine products include handicraft items such as carved statues and religious icons; household items such as the Tiffany lamps; jewelry made from gold, silver, brass and pearl; baskets, jars, vases. They include ready-to- wear dresses in the most modern fashions as well as knit wear and traditional clothes, the national costume made of cloth woven from banana fiber or pineapple fiber. World-famous Philippine furniture made from bamboo rattan or exquisitely carved wood can be priceless. Other items include snake or crocodile skin leather products, antiques and shell product. Virtually everything in the Philippines can be bought in Metro Manila. Just along the Tourist Belt, a tourist can acquire a wide variety of items from rows of specialty shops.

Like the culture in general, Filipino food is basically of Malay origin, with Spanish, Chinese, and American influences. Some standard dishes, such as the coconut-based ginattan, have retained their Malay origin. The most obvious Chinese contribution is noodles, which form the basis of the popular dishes. Regardless of origin, lechon lumpia, and pork adobo are now considered national dishes.

Regional variations in the fresh ingredients available account for provincial specialties. Among local specialties are lechon (suckling pig roasted over a charcoal pit and served with pork-liver sauce), adobo (marinated pork and chicken stew), kare-kare (chicken innards marinated in hot soup and stewed in peanut butter) and sinigang (a delicious sour soup). Tropical fruits are also delicious. During summer, try out halo-halo, a milkshake filled with fruit slices. San Miguel beer is both good and inexpensive.

English for Tourism

Tourist Information & Creative Thinking for Language Learners

CHAPTER 6

Philippines

Tourist Attractions | Unit 3

Vocabulary Practice

Which word does the following definition refer to?

1. *the quality of being liked or supported by a large number of people*

   a) population b) popularity

   c) proliferation d) heritage

2. *small island*

   a) icon b) islet

   c) archipelago d) peninsular

3. *the round open part of a volcano*

   a) plain b) crater

   c) ridge d) valley

4. *to expose oneself to pleasant warmth*

   a) lie b) show

   c) swim d) bask

5. *fall down*

   a) collapse b) occupy

   c) lie d) perch

Speaking Practice

How do you say the following in English?

1. 필리핀은 아시아태평양에 자리하고 있는 군도이다.

2. 홍콩이 북쪽의 이웃이다.

3. 더 북쪽에는 일본이 있다.

4. 서쪽에 싱가포르, 말레이시아, 태국이 놓여있다.

5. 필리핀을 구성하는 섬들은 잊혀진 섬들이다.

6. 대나무로 만들어진 필리핀 가구는 값을 매길 수 없을 정도로 값지다.

7. 상당한 수의 필리핀 사람들은 영어로 말한다.

8. 평균 온도는 24℃에서 31℃사이 이다.

9. Cebu는 Manila에서 비행기로 약 한 시간 거리에 있다.

10. 그 곳은 마닐라에서 차로 약 한 시간 거리에 있다.

Reading or Listening Practice

Boracay

Located at the northern tip of Panay island, Boracay is a tropical Island that is a one hour flight south of Manila. Boracay has charmed vacationers with its powder white sand, crystal blue waters. The island has more than 30 beaches, foremost of which is a four-kilometer stretch of pure white sand called White Beach. White Beach is widely considered by international travel publications to be among the world's best beaches.

Boracay is ideal for your tropical dream vacation. Numerous water sport facilities are on hand. Scuba divers will enjoy its dozens of dive spots and dive centers. One can learn wind surfing or kite boarding, go island-hopping, or simply bask in the never-ending sunshine. White Beach also has a stretch of establishments featuring an unprecedented variety of cuisines and cultures. Boracay is also well isolated and safe for children, and an excellent place for men and women to frolic and become children again!

Cebu

Cebu is the country's oldest and third largest city of the Philippines. It is about an hour flight from Manila and it is a city that blends its ancestral heritage and modern business. Standing as the country's top business and tourist destination, Cebu was called "Queen City of the South." Exploring Cebu City, one encounters a rich historic past.

Time has been kind to Cebu. From Zubu, the fishing village and busy trading port in 1521 has evolved a highly urbanized metropolitan center which now serves as focal point of growth and development in Southern Philippines. With its five cities (Cebu, Danao, Lapulapu Mandaue and Toledo) and its 48 smaller towns, Cebu has more than kept pace with the nation's progress. Today the island province has the highest economic growth rate anywhere in the country. Likewise, recent indications pointed out that Cebu has become the country's most favorite tourist destination.

In contrast to the bustling metropolis, the rest of Cebu's 167 islets and islands are lined with idyllic white sandy beaches and pristine clear waters. Cebu has gained wide popularity for its fantastic diving grounds evidenced by the proliferation of resorts which offer luxurious accommodations, excellent dive facilities and the services of competent dive masters and dive guides.

Tagaytay

With an altitude of 2,250 feet above sea level, Tagaytay City enjoys a cool climate all year round. This city perched on a ridge is located in the province of Cavite, some 56 kilometers south of Manila. It overlooks Manila Bay on the north, Taal Lake and Taal Volkano on the south, Laguna Bay, on the east and the China Sea on the west. The city is linked to the Metropolitan Manila and the province of Batangas by the Aguinaldo Highway.

Among its attractions is the Tagaytay Picnic Grove where one can get an unobstructed view of Taal Volcano, which lies within a lake. Taal Volcano, which rises 406 meters from the lake, is reputedly the world's smallest volcano. Taal Lake itself is an immense body of water formed when the old crater collapsed. For visiting tourists, Tagaytay is considered the 'sister' city of Las Vegas, Nevada, U.S.A; Tainan City, Taiwan; and Bankstown City, New South Wales, Australia.

Banaue

Banaue, 333 kilometers north of Manila, is one of the towns of the province of

Ifugao. Banaue derived its name from Banawol, a night bird that used to dwell in the area. A remote mountain community lives here. The beautiful rice terraces are the main attraction of this area. The terraces were hand- carved some 2,000 years ago using crude tools cutting into once barren rock, each ledge completely encompassing the mountain. The Ifugao tribes people who created and farmed the terraces in order to supply their staple crop of rice have in doing so left behind an architectural masterpiece. The fact that they were constructed using only primitive tools and bare hands makes the terraces even more astounding. The Banaue rice terraces are often referred to as the eighth wonder of the world (the first seven include the Pyramid of Giza, Hanging Gardens of Babylon, Statue of Zeus in Olympia, Temple of Artemis Ephesus, Tomb of Mausolus, Colossus of Rhodes, Pharoahs of Alexandria). They are the grandest man-made monuments of antiquity not made by slaves. It is believed that its length, if connected end to end would encircle half the globe. Now listed by UNESCO as World Heritage sites, they offer an unforgettable sight to tourists and trekkers in the area.

Going around Banaue involves walking up or down mountain paths. A visitor should wear comfortable footwear. The best time to see many wonders in Banaue if you want to see the green terraces is from April to August. Rainy season is from July to January, and cool months are from November to February.

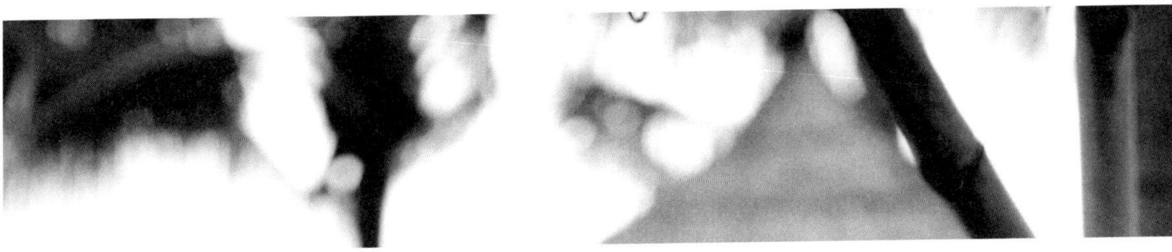

Answer Key

CHAPTER 1 China

Unit 1 Vocabulary & Grammar Practice

[1] b)

[2] a) farthest south
   b) of race
   c) of a different kind
   d) number of people living in a particular area
   e) an official process of counting a country's population
   f) connected with beauty
   g) large enough in amount or number to be noticeable
   h) land or district
   i) position of the rivers, roads, buildings, etc.
   j) free from extremes

[3] a) – h) b) – i) c) – j) d) – g) e) – a) f) – c) g) – b) h) – e) i) – f) j) – d)

Unit 2 Vocabulary & Grammar Practice

[1] b)

[2] b)

[3] a) – a) b) – c) c) – f) d) – h) e) – d) f) – e) g) – g) h) – i) i) – b) j) – j)

Unit 3 Vocabulary Practice

1. a) 2. b) 3. b) 4. a) 5. b)

Unit 3 Speaking Practice

1. Shanghai is located on the east coast of China.
2. Shanghai, which is located on the east coast of China, is the most populous city in China.
3. The Forbidden City was the imperial palace during the Ming and Qing dynasties.
4. The Forbidden City, which was the imperial palace during the Ming and Qing dynasties, is the largest palace in the world.
5. The Great Wall is considered one of the greatest wonders in the world.
6. The Great Wall, which is considered one of the greatest wonders in the world, was enlisted in the World Heritage by UNESCO in 1987.
7. The Summer Palace is the best preserved royal garden in China.
8. The Summer Palace, which is the best preserved royal garden, used to be a summer residence of Qing dynasty emperors.

9-10. It is said that Chinese eat everything that flies except planes, everything on the ground except cars, and everything in water except boats.

CHAPTER 2 Thailand

Unit 1 Vocabulary & Grammar Practice

[1] c)

[2] a) incapable of producing
b) of a countryside
c) of a town or city
d) able to produce good crops
e) something that is made to look like the original one
f) a type of pottery having a pale green glaze
g) a style of cooking
h) someone who sells things
i) a beautiful stone that has been cut into a special shape
j) extremely dry

[3] a) – b) b) – a) c) – j) d) – c) e) – d) f) – e) g) – h) h) – f) i) – g) j) – i)

Unit 2 Vocabulary & Grammar Practice

[1] a)

[2] a)

[3] a) – a) b) – b) c) – j) d) – d) e) – c) f) – h) g) – g) h) – f) i) – i) j) – e)

Unit 3 Vocabulary Practice

1. a) 2. d) 3. a) 4. b) 5. d)

Unit 3 Speaking Practice

1. Thailand was known as Siam.
2. Thailand, known as Siam, is located at the center of South East Asia.
3. Bangkok was established as a capital of Thailand.
4. Established as a capital of Thailand, Bangkok is the heart of the country, geographically and economically.
5. Pattaya is one of Thailand's biggest tourist destinations.
6. Pattaya, one of Thailand's biggest tourist destinations, is an ideal place for water sports.
7. Phuket is the largest island in Thailand.
8. Phuket, the largest island in Thailand, is a very attractive island for sightseeing.
9. Mini Siam is a theme park.
10. A theme park, Mini Siam, has scale models of Thailand' historical sites and temples.

CHAPTER 3 Malaysia

Unit 1 Vocabulary & Grammar Practice

[1] a)

[2] a) the end of something

b) a narrow passage of water that links two seas

c) join together to form one thing

d) place where two roads meet

e) to cut wood or stone into a shape

f) to make a hole through a piece of food

g) a drink made by mixing different things

h) a small shop with an open front

i) the flesh of lamb or sheep

j) a tool with a particular use in cooking

[3] a) – a) b) – d) c) – b) d) – c) e) – e) f) – j) g) – i) h) – f) i) – g) j) – h)

Unit 2 Vocabulary & Grammar Practice

[1] a)

[2] a)

[3] a) – d) b) – c) c) – e) d) – f) e) – j) f) – b) g) – i) h) – a) i) – h) j) – g)

Unit 3 Vocabulary Practice

1. a) 2. b) 3. c) 4. a) 5. d)

Unit 3 Speaking Practice

1. Malaysia is located in the heart of Southeast Asia.
2. Malaysia, located in the heart of Southeast Asia, is a multicultural society.
3. Malaysia is located at the southern tip of Malaysia.
4. Johor Bahru, located at the southern tip of Malaysia, is connected to Singapore by a causeway.
5. Penang has long been known as the Pearl of the Orient.
6. Penang known as the Pearl of the Orient is a tropical island resort.
7. The historical building in Malacca were built by the Dutch.
8. The temple has a seven-story pagoda.
9. Chinese comprise about a third of the population.
10. Days are very warm, while nights are fairly cool.

CHAPTER 4 Indonesia

Unit 1 Vocabulary & Grammar Practice

[1] c)

[2] a) a sharply pointed mountain top

b) treated animal skin used for making shoes, bags, etc.

c) group of many islands

d) to surround on all sides

e) a wide view of country scenery

f) to move from one place to another

g) a building in which Muslims worship

h) a large piece of land where crops are grown.

i) the heavy rains which fall in India and neighboring countries

j) to prevent from acting

[3] a) – a) b) – c) c) – d) d) – b) e) – g) f) – e) g) – j) h) – f) i) – i) j) – h)

Unit 2 Vocabulary & Grammar Practice

[1] a)

[2] c)

[3] a) – a) b) – e) c) – b) d) – f) e) – g) f) – c) g) – j) h) – d) i) – i) j) – h)

Unit 3 Vocabulary Practice

1. a) 2. b) 3. c) 4. b) 5. d)

Unit 3 Speaking Practice

1. Indonesia is the largest archipelago in the world.
2. Indonesia, the largest archipelago in the world, is the largest country in Southeast Asia.
3. The population of Indonesia is predominantly Muslims (Moslems).
4. Chinese restaurants are found all over the country.
5. Bali is based on Hinduism.
6. Indonesia is situated around the equator.
7. He always eats meals, watching TV.
8. Smiling at me, she shook hands with me.
9. Walking down the street, I met her.
10. Keeping pace with the number of visitors, more hotels have been built.

CHAPTER 5 Singapore

Unit 1 Vocabulary & Grammar Practice

[1] b)

[2] a) to move away or back
  b) free in action and behavior
  c) an object kept as a reminder of an event, trip, place, etc.
  d) an object produced or shaped by human beings
  e) small object that is valuable because it is old, beautiful, or rare
  f) an area away from the center of a town or city, where a lot of people live
  g) a store that sells the goods of a particular manufacturer or wholesaler
  h) someone who sells things in a shop
  i) offer made in reply to an offer made by somebody else
  j) having a pleasant smell

[3] a) – j) b) – i) c) – c) d) – h) e) – g) f) – f) g) – e) h) – d) i) – b) j) – a)

Unit 2 Vocabulary & Grammar Practice

[1] a)

[2] b)

[3] a) – f) b) – d) c) – a) d) – b) e) – h) f) – j) g) – c) h) – g) i) – e) j) – i)

Unit 3 Vocabulary Practice

1. a) 2. a) 3. c) 4. b) 5. b)

Unit 3 Speaking Practice

1. It is important to exercise regularly.
2. It is common for people to use 4 languages in Singapore.
3. Clarke Quay is Singapore's only riverside village.
4. Clarke Quay is Singapore's only riverside village combining dining, shopping, and entertainment.
5. Clarke Quay was named after Governor Clarke.
6. Named after Singapore's Governor Clarke, Clarke Quay was the center of commerce.
7. Sentosa Island is Singapore's mega theme-park.
8. Sentosa Island is Singapore's mega theme-park, attracting numerous visitors every year.
9. Underwater World has been praised as Asia's most exciting tropical ocenarium.
10. Praised as Asia's most exciting tropical oceanarium, Under World has a 80-meter transparent tunnel.

CHAPTER 6 Philippines

Unit 1 Vocabulary & Grammar Practice

[1] d)

[2] a) a native or inhabitant of the Philippines
    b) the Filipino language
    c) fairly large in amount, size, or degree
    d) figure of a person, animal, etc. in wood, stone, bronze, etc.
    e) to take possession of a country
    f) to take the skin off
    g) to take the vows of a religious order
    h) material formed by weaving
    i) the act or action of teaching
    j) pass across

[3] a) – j) b) – b) c) – a) d) – h) e) – i) f) – c) g) – d) h) – f) i) – g) j) – e)

Unit 2 Vocabulary & Grammar Practice

[1] d)

[2] d)

[3] a) – a) b) – c) c) – b) d) – e) e) – d) f) – j) g) – f) h) – h) i) – g) j) – i)

Unit 3 Vocabulary Practice

1. a) 2. b) 3. b) 4. d) 5. a)

Unit 3 Speaking Practice

1. The Philippines is an archipelago situated in the Asia Pacific.
2. Hong Kong is a northern neighbor.
3. Further north is Japan.
4. To the west lies Singapore, Malaysia, and Thailand.
5. The islands that comprise the Philippines are the forgotten islands.
6. Philippine furniture made from bamboo are priceless.
7. A considerable number of Filipinos speak English.
8. Average temperatures range from 24℃ to 31℃.
9. Cebu is about an hour flight from Manila.
10. The place is about an hour drive from Manila.

REFERENCES

Seong, Myeong-Hee.(2004). Practical Tourism English Reading. Seoul: Baeksan Publishing Co.

Seong, Myeong-Hee.(2011). Travel English. Seoul: Baeksan Publishing Co.

Seong, Myeong-Hee. & Klemsen, K. M.(2014). Resort & Sports English. Seoul: Baeksan Publishing Co.

http://www.en.wikipedia.org

http://www.en.wikipedia.org/wiki/China

http://www.en.wikipedia.org/wiki/Thailand

http://www.en.wikipedia.org/wiki/Malaysia

http://www.en.wikipedia.org/wiki/Indonesia

http://www.en.wikipedia.org/wiki/Singapore

http://www.en.wikipedia.org/wiki/Philippines